Barcelona

Micha Pawlitzki **Barcelona**

EDITION**PANORAMA**BIBLIOTHEK

Barcelona

Iris Lemanczyk

Die Sonne steigt aus dem Meer. Sie taucht La Rambla, die am Tag quirlende Lebensader der katalanischen Metropole, in blau schimmerndes Licht. Ein Schauspiel, das den Geist wachstreichelt. Aus dicken Schläuchen spritzen die Männer der Reinigungskolonne Wasser. Sie putzen die Hinterlassenschaften der Nacht aus den Winkeln der Flaniermeile, machen sie fein für den neuen Tag. Im Untergrund grollt die erste Metro. Die letzten Nachtschwärmer suchen den Heimweg.

Wenn der Tag in Barcelona überhaupt einen Anfang hat, dann beginnt er morgens um halb fünf in der Boqueria, der Markthalle der Innenstadt. „Platz, auf dem Ziegenbockfleisch verkauft wird", soll Boqueria, ein altes katalanisches Wort, bedeuten. Heute wird nicht nur Ziegenfleisch feil geboten. Unter dem eisernen Dach ist auch einer der größten Fischmärkte Europas zu Haus. Von hier aus wandern tagtäglich Tonnen von Meeresgetier in die Töpfe und Pfannen der genussfreudigen Barcelonier. Tausend Gerüche, mal angenehm, aber auch mal zum Nase rümpfen, wecken in diesem Bauch Barcelonas Appetit oder zumindest Neugierde: Muscheln, Garnelen und Langusten oder Schweinepfoten, Blutwurst, Speck und Suppenhühner oder Trüffeln. Kanarische Bananen, Oliven, Pistazien, Saubohnen und Tomaten oder Tauben, Kaninchen, Stockfische und silberne Riesenaale. In der Boqueria ist jede Kundin - sei sie 17 oder 70 Jahre alt - eine Königin, Prinzessin oder ein Kindchen. Männer werden mit „Mein Herzblut" oder „Mein Schöner" angeredet. Mittendrin, am Tapas-Stand „Pinocho", treffen sich frühmorgens die Köche der guten Restaurants auf einen café con leche und beraten über die Angebote des Tages.

Mittlerweile schminken sich die ersten Straßenkünstler auf der Rambla. Und verwandeln sich mit verschwenderischen Kostümen in stille, fast bewegungslose Engel, Könige, Indianer oder in Batman. Kartenleser warten auf Kundschaft, Pantomimen, Feuerschlucker, Jongleure und Musiker nutzen die schattige Platanenallee als Bühne. Zwölfhundert Meter Laufsteg, Gedränge, Furcht vor Taschendieben, Happening, Mulitkulti, brüllende Händler, undefinierbarer Lärm, versprengte Augenblicke ...

Rambla bedeutet ausgetrocknetes Flussbett, das als Weg benutzt wird. Genau das war auch La Rambla. Mit dem Abriss der Stadtmauer entstanden dort die ersten Adelspaläste, im 19. Jahrhundert wurden die Platanen gepflanzt, die so viel zur angenehmen Atmosphäre beitragen. Wobei die Rambla aus mehreren Abschnitten besteht: die Rambla de Canaletes, die Rambla dels Estudis, die Rambla Sant Josep, die Rambla dels Caputxins und die Rambla Santa Mònica.

Um den eisernen Brunnen Font de Canaletes auf der Rambla de Canaletes scharen sich wochentags von zwölf bis eins die Pensionäre. Wie die um die Papierkörbe tippelnden Tauben picken sie sich die neuesten Ergebnisse, Gerüchte und Zeitungsmeldungen über ihren Fußballclub, den FC Barcelona, heraus. Sie diskutieren, spekulieren und teilen miteinander - wenn sie am Ende den Vorsprung vor Real Madrid ausrechnen - das wohlige Gefühl von Zufriedenheit. Die Freude der Fans ist nicht nur sportlicher Natur, denn jeder Sieg von „Barça" auf dem Fußballplatz ist zugleich ein Triumph der Autonomen Region Katalonien über Madrid. Hier geht es um Ehre und Schmach. Mehr als alles andere ist der Klub Symbol für den Kampf der Katalanen gegen die Zentralregierung in Madrid. Die Liga nicht zu gewinnen, ist schlimm, hinter Real Madrid zu landen eine Katastrophe. Im Stadion kommt deswegen vor allem im

Match gegen den Erzrivalen der „Barcelonismus“ voll zum Tragen, jene Mischung aus weltoffenem Unabhängigkeitsstreben und chauvinistischem Dünkel, geheimnisvoll gemixt mit „seny“, dem gesunden Menschenverstand, und „rauxa“, dem kreativen Chaos, aber auch der Hitzköpfigkeit und Heiterkeit.

Wenn „rauxa“ tatsächlich für die Kreativität verantwortlich ist, dann ist Barcelona reichlich damit gesegnet. Wie eine Zauberin wandelt die Stadt unermüdlich ihr Gesicht. Bei zwei Weltausstellungen und den Olympischen Spielen von 1992 nutzte Barcelona jedes Mal die Chance, über ihre Grenzen hinaus zu wachsen, überalterte Viertel zu erneuern und sich in neuem Glanz herauszuputzen. Diese Dichte! Dieses Tempo! Wer die Stadt vor den Spielen erlebt hat, reibt sich die Augen. In der südlichsten Stadt des Nordens oder der nördlichsten Stadt des Südens vereinen sich mediterrane Lebensfreude mit großstädtischer Produktivität. Und dabei setzt die Natur Barcelona enge Grenzen. Eingezwängt zwischen Meer, dem Hausberg Montjuïc und den Ausläufern der Serra de Collserola ist der Siedlungsraum knapp bemessen.

Besonders viel „rauxa“ steckt im Viertel Eixample und in den Bauwerken Antoni Gaudís. Im Laufe des 19. Jahrhunderts drohte Barcelona aus allen Nähten zu platzen. Die Stadt begann sich auszudehnen, bis sie fast die gesamte Ebene einnahm, die sich, sanft abfallend, von den Bergen bis zum Meer erstreckte. „Eixample“, Stadterweiterung, nannte man das neue Viertel, ein nüchterner Name für das, was später der charakteristischste Teil Barcelonas werden sollte. Der Ingenieur Ildefons Cerdà entwarf ein Viertel mit Schachbrettmuster aus breiten, sich im rechten Winkel kreuzenden Straßen. Das reiche Bürgertum baute hier, um der Enge der Altstadt zu entrinnen.

Dann passierte etwas Unerwartetes. Wenige Jahre nach dem Beginn der Bauarbeiten – im späten 19. Jahrhundert – erwachte in der Stadt ein neuer Architekturstil, der in Barcelona als Modernisme, im übrigen Europa als Art nouveau, Jugendstil oder Modern Style seinen Siegeszug antrat. Der Modernisme lässt sich ausgerechnet im strengen, rationalen Grundriss des Eixample nieder. Fantasievoll, übermütig, organisch, voll magischer Kurven, Schnörkeln, Ornamenten und träumerischen Farben. Eine steinerne Fantasiewelt. Bunt und verspielt.

Im Eixample, wo es den Bewohnern aus Prestigegründen verboten ist, die Wäsche zur Straßenseite hin aufzuhängen, steht wohl der berühmteste Bau des Modernisme: die Sagrada Família, die Kirche der Heiligen Familie. Die Unvollendete. Die rein aus privaten Spenden finanzierte Kirche wird 1882 als konventionell neogotischer Bau begonnen. Ein Jahr später übernimmt der gerade 31-jährige Antoni Gaudí die architektonische Leitung und verändert die Pläne wieder und wieder. Die Kirche wird zu seinem Lebenswerk, soll zu einer „Predigt aus Stein“ werden. Ab 1911 lehnt Gaudí alle weiteren Aufträge ab und konzentriert sich ausschließlich auf die Sagrada Família, lebt auf der Baustelle. Lebt für die Baustelle. 43 Jahre lang. Gaudí kann, nach Kryta und Apsis, nur die gewaltige, von Figuren überquellende Ostfassade sowie die vier 110 Meter hohen Türme vollenden. 1926 wird Gaudí von einer Straßenbahn erfasst und stirbt, weil die Erste Hilfe ausbleibt. Wegen seiner abgenutzten Kleidung erkennt man den Baumeister zu spät.

Unterbrochen durch den Spanischen Bürgerkrieg werden die Bauarbeiten 1952 wieder aufgenommen. Gaudí soll mit einer Bauzeit von 200 Jahren gerechnet haben. Optimisten hoffen, dass die Arbeiten bis 2020, vielleicht aber auch erst 2040 abgeschlossen sein werden. Lange galten Gaudís Bauwerke bei den Einheimischen allenfalls als Kuriositäten der Architekturgeschichte. Erst durch das rege Interesse vor allem japanischer Touristen gewann der Meister des katalonischen Jugendstils bei den Barceloniern neues Ansehen.

Wenn die Rambla die Hauptschlagader der Stadt ist und Eixamples die Vistenkarte des Modernisme, dann ist das Barri Gòtic das Herz Barcelonas. Hier gründeten die Römer ihre „colònia“, ihre Stadt, seitdem befindet sich die Stadtverwaltung hier. Friedlich döst eine Katze in der Sonne, genießt die Wärme der Mauersteine. Seifensieder, Hutmacher, Goldschmiede, daneben kleine Bars, Bäckereien und Cafés - in den engen Gassen kann man sich verlieren, trotzdem geht es gemütlich zu. Gemütlich, aber nicht museal. Trotz des Königspalastes, in dem 1493 Kolumbus empfangen wurde, als er von seiner Entdeckungsreise in die Neue Welt zurückgekehrt war. Und trotz der gotischen Kathedrale, in deren Taufbecken sechs Indios getauft wurden, die der Entdecker von seiner Reise mitgebracht hatte.

Glücklich, wer die Fassade der Kathedrale zu Gesicht bekommt. Versteckt sie sich doch meist hinter Baugerüsten. Vor dem Hauptportal der Kathedrale wird meist an Sonntagvormittagen die Sardana getanzt. Die Tanzlustigen fassen sich an den Händen und bewegen sich im Kreis in kleinen Schritten fast unmerklich von der Stelle. Platz ist für Touristen genauso wie für Barcelonier. Während der Franco-Ära war der Tanz verboten, weil in ihm die katalanische Zusammengehörigkeit ihren Ausdruck findet.

Getanzt wurde trotzdem, denn Anarchie ist Teil der Stadtgeschichte. Am 19. Juli 1936 sollten in Barcelona eigentlich die Olympischen Spiele eröffnet werden. Die Antwort der europäischen Linken auf die in Berlin stattfindende Olympiade. Doch im Morgengrauen erhebt sich das Volk gegen die Truppen des Generalísimo Franco – der Bürgerkrieg beginnt. Im zweitägigen, blutigen Straßenkampf gelingt es den Arbeitern unter Führung des legendären Buenaventura Durruti, die putschenden Militärs niederzuschlagen. Einen Sommer lang herrscht die anarchistische Gewerkschaft CNT, die Confederación Nacional del Trabajo, in der fast alle Arbeiter der Stadt organisiert sind. Sie werden danach unter Franco rigoros verfolgt, aber die Erinnerung an die Euphorie und die Ideale dieser Zeit bleibt bis heute lebendig.

Älter, viel älter als die Eixamples, ist der Stadtteil Barceloneta auf einer Landzunge des Hafenbeckens. Das Viertel entstand 1719, als der Bourbonenkönig Philipp V. eine Zitadelle haben wollte. Die Bewohner wurden nach Barceloneta zwangsumgesiedelt. Seitdem wohnen hier hauptsächlich Fischer und Hafenarbeiter. Man kennt sich. Kannte sich. Denn immer mehr vermögende Fremde entdecken den Reiz von Barceloneta und lassen sich auf der Landzunge nieder.

Für die Olympischen Spiele öffnete sich Barcelona hin zum Meer, und Barceloneta bekam einen kilometerlangen Sandstrand, der vormittags von braun gegerbten Rentnern bevölkert wird, die sich an Campingtischen Schachduelle liefern.

Auf der Strandpromenade bummeln junge Mütter zum Olympischen Dorf mit seinem Markenzeichen, der Skulptur einer riesigen, gestrandeten Sardine, deren aus Bronzedraht gefertigte Schuppen in der Sonne leuchten. Ein Werk des Architekten Frank Gehry. Dominiert wird das Dorf von den beiden höchsten Häusern Spaniens: der Versicherungsanstalt Mapfre und dem Hotel Arts. Noch bis in die 1980er Jahre sah die Küste völlig anders aus, war Industriegebiet. Damals konnten die Barcelonier von einem Hausstrand, von Palmen, von Bars und Cafés direkt am Meer nur träumen.

Im Hafen steht auch die Torre de Sant Sebastià, die rote Seilbahn, die quer übers Hafenbecken zum Montjuïc führt, Barcelonas „Haushügel“ und die größte Grünfläche weit und breit. Gleichzeitig war der Montjuïc auch immer Barcelonas „hochmütige Mutter“, wie es der katalanische Poet Jacint Verdaguer ausdrückte: Aus den zahllosen Steinbrüchen am Montjuïc stammt das Material für Barcelonas Stadtmauern, Häuser und Kirchen. Zur Weltausstellung 1929 wurden Parks und monumentale Museen wie das Palau Nacional, das heutige Museum für katalanische Kunst, errichtet. Dazu noch Sportanlagen, Theater und Freilichtbühnen. Der Hügel mauserte sich zum Naherholungsgebiet, zur grünen Lunge. Aber den schönsten Ausblick über Barcelona bietet sich nicht vom Montjuïc, sondern vom märchenhaften Parc Güell, der Teil einer von Gaudí gestalteten Wohnanlage werden sollte. Doch das Geld wurde knapp. Geblieben ist ein verträumter Park mit Säulen und Skulpturen und einer langen Schlangenbank aus bunter Bruchkeramik. Von fern sind die Türme der Sagrada Família zu sehen, die geordneten Straßen von Eixamples und die grünen Blätter der Platanen auf der Rambla. Meer, Strand, Bäume, Häuser, Mosaike – alles glänzt. Barcelona strahlt im satten Licht des frühen Abends. Zwischen Meer und Bergen liegt die Stadt eingefasst wie ein Juwel. In Stein gehauene Geschichte und moderne Metropole voller Lebenslust. Rund um die Uhr.

Barcelona

Iris Lemanczyk

El sol surt pel mar. Amb una llum blava respendent banya la Rambla, l'artèria vital de la metròpoli catalana agitada durant el dia. Un espectacle que desperta suaument l'esperit. L'aigua brolla a dojo de les mànegues gruixudes de la brigada de la neteja. Netejen el llegat de la nit dels racons del passeig, l'enllesteixen per a un nou dia. Al subsòl retruny el primer metro. Els últims noctàmbuls emprenen el camí cap a casa.

Si a Barcelona el dia hagués de tenir un inici, aquest començaria a dos-quarts de cinc a la Boqueria, el mercat del casc antic. Sembla que boqueria, una paraula catalana arcaica, vol dir «plaça on es ven carn de boc». Avui dia no tan sols s'hi ven aquesta carn. Sota aquesta teulada de ferro s'hi troba un dels mercats de peix més grans d'Europa. Des d'aquí, dia rere dia surten tones de bestioles marines camí de les cassoles i paelles dels barcelonins *bon vivants*. Milers d'olors, a vegades agradables, però que a vegades també fan arrufar el nas, desperten en aquesta panxa de Barcelona si no la gana, almenys, la curiositat: musclos, gambes i llagostes o peus de porc, botifarra negra, cansalada i pollastre per al brou o tòfona. Plàtans de Canàries, olives, festucs i tomàquets o coloms, conills, bacallà i anguiles gegants platejades. A la Boqueria, cada clienta (ja tingui 17 anys o 70) és una reina, una princesa o una nena. Als homes s'hi dirigeixen amb un «xato» o «guapo». Al bell mig del mercat, al bar de tapes Pinotxo, els cuiners dels bons restaurants es troben a primera hora del matí fent un cafè amb llet mentre conversen sobre les ofertes del dia.

Mentrestant, els primers artistes de carrer es maquillen a la Rambla. I amb disfresses fastuoses es transformen en àngels, reis, indis o Batmans callats, gairebé immòbils. Els lectors de tarot esperen clientela; pantomims, faquirs, malabaristes i músics fan servir l'ombrívol passeig de plàtans com a escenari. Mil dos-cents metres de passarel·la, gentada, temor pels carteristes, happenings, multiculturalitat, venedors cridaners, soroll indefinible, moments dispersos...

Rambla vol dir llit de riu assecat que es fa servir de camí. I justament això era la Rambla. Amb l'enderrocament de les muralles van alçar-se els primers palaus senyorials, el segle XIX es van plantar els primers plàtans que tant contribueixen a crear aquesta atmosfera tan agradable. Per cert, la Rambla està composta de diversos trams. la Rambla de Canaletes, la Rambla dels Estudis, la Rambla de Sant Josep, la Rambla dels Caputxins i la Rambla de Santa Mònica.

Vora la Font de Canaletes, de ferro i situada a la Rambla de Canaletes, es reuneixen entre setmana de dotze a una els jubilats. Com els coloms que saltironegen per les papereres, esgranen els resultats, rumors i notícies del diari més recents sobre el seu club de futbol, el FC Barcelona. Discuteixen, especulen i comparteixen (si al final compten amb avantatge respecte del Real Madrid) la sensació agradable de satisfacció. L'alegria dels aficionats no és només de caire esportiu, cada victòria del Barça al camp de futbol és, al mateix temps, un triomf de Catalunya sobre Madrid. Va

d'honor i d'infàmia. Més que cap altra cosa, el club és símbol de la lluita dels catalans contra el govern central de Madrid. No guanyar la lliga és dolent, acabar darrere del Real Madrid, una catàstrofe. Per això, a l'estadi, sobretot al partit contra l'arxirival, el barcelonisme posa en acció aquella mescla d'aspiracions d'independentisme cosmopolita i presumpció nacionalista, barrejat misteriosament amb el seny, el sentit comú sa, i la rauxa, el caos creatiu, però també amb el fanatisme i la jovialitat.

Si la rauxa realment és responsable de la creativitat, aleshores Barcelona ha estat beneïda en escreix. Com una fetillera, la ciutat transforma incansablement la seva cara. Per les dues Exposicions Universals i pels Jocs Olímpics de 1992, Barcelona va aprofitar cada vegada l'oportunitat per créixer més enllà dels seus límits, rehabilitar barris envellits i per enllustrar-se de nou. Quina densitat! Quin ritme! Qui coneixia la ciutat abans dels Jocs, ara es frega els ulls. A la ciutat més meridional del nord o a la ciutat més septentrional del sud s'uneixen la vitalitat mediterrània amb la productivitat de les metròpolis. I això que la natura marca uns límits estrets a Barcelona. Encaixonada entre el mar, la muntanya de Montjuïc i els vessants de la serra de Collserola, l'espai ocupable està calculat mil·limètricament.

Molta rauxa és el que especialment es troba a l'Eixample i als edificis d'Antoni Gaudí. Al llarg del segle XIX, Barcelona amenaçava rebentar per totes les costures. La ciutat es va començar a expandir fins a ocupar gairebé tota la plana que s'estenia, caient suaument, de les muntanyes fins al mar. El nou barri fou anomenat Eixample, un nom sobri pel que més tard seria la part més característica de Barcelona. L'enginyer Ildefons Cerdà va dissenyar un barri com un tauler d'escacs fet de carrers amples que formen angles rectes. La burgesia rica hi va construir per fugir de l'estretor del casc antic.

Aleshores va passar quelcom d'inesperat. Pocs anys després del començament de les obres, a finals del segle XIX, va despertar a la ciutat un nou estil arquitectònic, que a Barcelona va fer la seva entrada triomfal com a Modernisme i a la resta d'Europa com a Art Noveau, Jugendstil o Modern Style. El modernisme es va establir precisament a la planta estricta i racional de l'Eixample. Imaginatiu, entremaliat, orgànic, ple de corbes màgiques, volutes, ornaments i colors de somni. Un món imaginari de pedra. Multicolor i juganer.

A l'Eixample, on, per motius de prestigi, als veïns no els és permès d'estendre la roba a la façana del carrer, hi ha segurament l'edifici més conegut del modernisme: la Sagrada Família. La inacabada. L'església, finançada tan sols amb donatius privats, es va començar a construir el 1882 com una construcció neogòtica convencional. Un any més tard, Antoni Gaudí, amb només 31 anys, assumeix la direcció arquitectònica i modifica els plànols una i una altra vegada. L'església esdevé l'obra de la seva vida, havia de ser un «sermó de pedra». A partir de 1911, Gaudí refusa la resta dels encàrrecs i es concentra exclusivament en la Sagrada Família, viu a l'obra. Viu per a l'obra. Durant 43 anys. Després de la cripta i l'absis, només pot completar la imponent façana est, desbordada de figures, així com les quatre torres de 110 metres. El 1926 un tramvia atropella Gaudí i mor per manca de primers auxilis. Com que duia roba gastada, reconeixen el mestre d'obres massa tard.

Interrompudes per la Guerra Civil espanyola, les obres es reprenen el 1952. Es diu que Gaudí calculava que la construcció duraria 200 anys. Els optimistes esperen que les tasques acabin el 2020 però potser no finalitzaran fins el 2040. Durant molt de temps, els barcelonins van considerar les obres de Gaudí curiositats de la història de l'arquitectura. No va ser fins que va despertar l'interès sobretot dels turistes japonesos que el mestre del modernisme català va guanyar una nova consideració entre els barcelonins.

Si la Rambla és l'aorta de la ciutat i l'Eixample la targeta de visita del modernisme, llavors el Barri Gòtic és el cor de Barcelona. Aquí, els romans van fundar la seva «colònia», la seva ciutat, des d'aleshores l'administració municipal es troba aquí. Un gat dormisqueja tranquil·lament al sol, gaudeix de la calor de les totxanes. Saboners, barretaires, orfebres, al costat de petits bars, fleques i cafès (un es pot perdre pels carrerons estrets, però se'n surt agradablement). És agradable, però no és museístic. Malgrat el Palau Reial on Colom fou rebut el 1943 en tornar del seu viatge de descobriment del Nou Món. I malgrat la catedral gòtica a la pica baptismal de la qual foren batejats sis indis que el descobridor va portar del seu viatge.

Qui pot arribar a veure la façana de la catedral pot considerar-se afortunat. Gairebé sempre s'amaga darrere de bastides. Davant de la portalada principal de la catedral, sobretot els diumenges el matí, es ballen sardanes. Els amants de la dansa s'agafen les mans i es van movent gairebé impreceptiblement del lloc fent petits passos amb cercle. De lloc n'hi ha tant per als turistes com per als barcelonins. A l'època de Franco la dansa fou prohibida per ser l'expressió del sentiment de pertinença català.

Això no obstant, es ballava, i és que l'anarquia és part de la història de la ciutat. De fet, el 19 de juliol de 1936 s'havien d'inaugurar els Jocs Olímpics a Barcelona. La resposta de l'esquerra europea a l'olimpíada celebrada a Berlín. Però a l'alba, el poble s'aixeca contra les tropes del General Franco. Comença la Guerra Civil. Amb dos dies de lluita sagnant als carrers, els treballadors, sota la direcció del llegendari Buenaventura Durriti, aconsegueixen derrotar els militars colpistes. El sindicat anarquista CNT, Confederació Nacional del Treball, a l'entorn del qual s'han organitzat gairebé tots els treballadors de la ciutat, domina tot l'estiu. Posteriorment són rigurosament perseguits per Franco, però el record de l'eufòria i dels ideals d'aquells dies han restat vius fins avui.

Més antic, molt més antic que l'Eixample, és el barri de la Barceloneta que es troba en una llengua de la dàrsena. El barri es va construir el 1719, quan el Borbó Felip V volia una ciutadella. Els habitants van ser desplaçats a la força cap a la Barceloneta. Des d'aleshores aquí hi viuen majoritàriament pescadors i treballadors del port. La gent es conelx. O es coneixia. I és que cada vegada més forasters acomodats descobreixen l'atractlu de la Barceloncta i s'estableixen en aquesta llengua de terra.

Pels Jocs Olímpis, Barcelona es va obrir al mar i la Barceloneta va obtenir una platja d'un quilòmetre de llarg, que els matins es pobla de jubilats curtits pel sol que disputen duels d'escacs en taules de càmping.

Pel passeig marítim passegen mares joves camí de la Vila Olímpica, amb el seu símbol, l'escultura d'una sardina gegant embarrancada, les escames de filament de bronze de la qual brillen amb el sol. Una obra de l'arquitecte Frank Gehry. Els dos edificis més alts d'Espanya dominen la Vila Olímpica: el de l'asseguradora Mapfre i el de l'Hotel Arts. Però fins els anys vuitanta la costa presentava un altre aspecte, era una zona industrial. En aquella època els barcelonins només podien fer que somiar una casa de platja, amb palmeres, bars i cafès tocant el mar.

Al port també hi ha la Torre de Sant Sebastià, el telefèric vermell que creua el port fins a Montjuïc, la muntanya local de Barcelona, i la zona verda més gran a la rodona. Al mateix temps, Montjuïc sempre va ser la «matrona», amb paraules del poeta català Jacint Verdaguer: de les nombroses canteres de Montjuïc prové el material de les muralles de Barcelona, cases i esglésies. Per l'Exposició Universal de 1929 es van edificar parcs i museus monumentals com el Palau Nacional, avui, Museu Nacional d'Art de Catalunya. I a més també instal·lacions esportives, teatres i escenaris a l'aire lliure. El turó es va convertir en àrea de repòs local, en pulmó verd. Això no obstant, la millor vista de Barcelona no l'ofereix Montjuïc, sinó el tabulós Parc Güell, que havia de ser una zona residencial ideada per Gaudí. Però els diners van escassejar. N'ha quedat un parc somniador amb columnes i escultures i un llarg banc en forma de serp amb trencadís de colors. De la llunyania es poden veure les torres de la Sagrada Família, els carrers ordenats de l'Eixample, les fulles verdes dels plàtans de la Rambla. Mar, platja, arbres, cases, mosaics: tot brilla. Barcelona llueix a la llum saturada de primera hora del vespre. Entre el mar i les muntanyes hi trobem la ciutat, incrustada com una joia. Història escolpida a pedra i metròpoli moderna plena de vitalitat. No s'atura mai.

Barcelona

Iris Lemanczyk

El sol sale por el mar. Una luz azul resplandeciente baña La Rambla, la arteria vital, agitada durante el día, de la metrópoli catalana. Un espectáculo que despierta suavemente el espíritu. El agua sale a chorro de las gruesas mangueras de la brigada de la limpieza. Limpian el legado de la noche de los rincones del paseo, lo arreglan para un nuevo día. En el subsuelo retumba el primer metro. Los últimos noctámbulos toman el camino a casa.

Si en Barcelona el día tuviera que tener un inicio, éste empezaría a las cuatro y media en La Boqueria, el mercado del centro histórico. Parece que boqueria, una antigua palabra catalana, significa «plaza donde se vende carne de macho cabrío». Hoy en día no sólo se vende este tipo de carne. Bajo este tejado de hierro se encuentra uno de los mercados de pescado más grandes de Europa. De aquí, día tras día salen toneladas de bichos marinos camino de los pucheros y sartenes de los barceloneses *bon vivants*. Miles de olores, a veces agradables, pero que a veces también hacen arrugar la nariz, despiertan en esta barriga de Barcelona si no el hambre, por lo menos sí la curiosidad: mejillones, gambas y langostas o manitas de cerdo, butifarra negra, tocino y pollo para el caldo o trufa. Plátanos de Canarias, aceitunas, pistachos y tomates o palomas, conejos, bacalao y anguilas gigantes plateadas. En La Boqueria, cada clienta, (tenga 17 o 70 años) es una reina, una princesa o una nena. A los hombres se dirigen con un «corazón» o un «guapo». Justo en el centro del mercado, en el bar de tapas Pinocho, los cocineros de los buenos restaurantes se encuentran a primera hora de la mañana tomando un café con leche y conversan acerca de las ofertas del día.

Mientras, los primeros artistas de calle se maquillan en La Rambla. Y con disfraces fastuosos se transforman en ángeles, reyes, indios o Batmans callados, casi inmóviles. Los lectores de tarot esperan clientes; pantomimos, faquires, malabaristas y músicos utilizan este sombreado paseo de plátanos como escenario. Mil dos-cientos metros de pasarela, gentío, temor por los carteristas, happenings, multiculturalidad, griterío de vendedores, ruido indefinible, momentos dispersos...

Rambla significa lecho de río seco que se usa como camino. Precisamente eso era La Rambla. Tras el derribo de las murallas se irguieron los primeros palacios señoriles, en el siglo XIX se plantaron los primeros plátanos que tanto contribuyen a crear esa atmósfera agradable. Por cierto, La Rambla está compuesta por varios tramos: La Rambla de Canaletes, La Rambla dels Estudis, La Rambla de Sant Josep, La Rambla dels Caputxins y La Rambla de Santa Mònica.

Alrededor de la Fuente de Canaletes, de hierro y situada en La Rambla de Canaletes, se reúnen entre semana de doce a una los jubilados. Como las palomas que dan saltitos por las papeleras, desgranan los resultados, rumores y noticias del periódico más recientes sobre su club de fútbol, el FC Barcelona. Discuten, especulan y comparten (si al final cuentan con ventaja con respecto al Real Madrid) la agradable sensación de satisfacción. La alegría de los seguidores no sólo tiene un cariz deportivo, cada victoria del Barça en la cancha es, al mismo tiempo, un triunfo de Cataluña sobre Madrid. Va de honor e infamia. Más que cualquier otra cosa, el club es símbolo de la lucha de los catalanes contra el gobierno central de Madrid. No ganar la liga es malo, acabar por detrás del Real Madrid, una catástrofe. Por eso, en el estadio, sobretodo en el partido contra el archirival, el barcelonismo hace alarde de esa mezcla de aspiraciones de independentismo cosmopolita y presunción nacionalista, a lo que se añade misteriosamente el *seny,* el sano juicio, y la *rauxa*, el caos creativo, pero también el fanatismo y la jovialidad.

Si realmente es la *rauxa* la responsable de la creatividad, entonces Barcelona ha resultado bendecida con creces. Como una hechicera, la ciudad transforma su rostro incansablemente. Con motivo de las dos Exposiciones Universales y los Juegos Olímpicos de 1992, Barcelona aprovechó siempre la oportunidad para crecer más allá de sus límites, rehabilitar barrios envejecidos y lustrarlos nuevamente. ¡Qué densidad! ¡Qué ritmo! Quien conocía la ciudad antes de los Juegos, ahora se frota los ojos. En la ciudad más meridional del norte o la más septentrional del sur se unen la vitalidad mediterránea con la productividad de las metrópolis. Y eso pese a que la naturaleza marca unos límites estrechos a Barcelona. Encajonada entre el mar, la montaña de Montjuïc y las laderas de la sierra de Collserola, el espacio ocupable está calculado milimétricamente.

Mucha *rauxa* es lo que se encuentra especialmente en el Eixample y en los edificios de Antoni Gaudí. A lo largo del siglo XIX Barcelona amenazaba reventar por todas sus costuras. La ciudad empezó a expandirse hasta ocupar casi toda la llanura que se extendía, cayendo suavemente, de las montañas hasta el mar. Eixample (ensanche) fue el nombre que recibió el nuevo barrio, un nombre sobrio para lo que más tarde sería la parte más característica de Barcelona. El ingeniero Ildefons Cerdà diseñó un barrio a modo de tablero de ajedrez a base de calles anchas conformando ángulos rectos. La rica burguesía construyó allí huyendo de la estrechez del barrio antiguo.

Entonces ocurrió algo inesperado. A los pocos años del inicio de las obras, a finales del siglo XIX, empezó a despuntar en la ciudad un nuevo estilo arquitectónico que en Barcelona entró triunfalmente como Modernismo y en el resto de Europa como Art Noveau, Jugendstil o Modern Style. El modernismo se estableció precisamente en la planta estricta y racional del Eixample. Imaginativo, travieso, orgánico, repleto de curvas mágicas, volutas, ornamentos y colores de ensueño. Un mundo imaginario de piedra. Multicolor y juguetón.

En el Eixample, donde, por motivos de prestigio, los vecinos no pueden tender la ropa en la fachada que da a la calle, seguramente está el edificio más conocido del modernismo: la Sagrada Família. La inacabada. La iglesia, financiada solamente con donativos privados, se empezó a construir en 1882 como construcción neogótica convencional. Un año más tarde, Antoni Gaudí, con sólo 31 años, asumió la dirección arquitectónica y modificó los planos una y otra vez. La iglesia se convirtió en la obra de su vida, tenía que ser un «sermón de piedra». A partir de 1911, Gaudí rechaza el resto de encargos y se concentra exclusivamente en la Sagrada Família, vive en la obra. Vive para la obra. Durante 43 años. Después de la cripta y el ábside, sólo pudo completar la imponente fachada este, rebosante de figuras, así como las cuatro torres de 110 metros. En 1926 un tranvía atropelló a Gaudí y murió al no recibir primeros auxilios. Como llevaba ropa muy usada, reconocieron al maestro de obras demasiado tarde.

Las obras, que fueron interrumpidas por la Guerra Civil española, se retoman en 1952. Se dice que Gaudí calculaba que la construcción duraría 200 años. Los optimistas esperan que ésta concluya en 2020 pero tal vez no lo haga hasta el 2040. Por mucho tiempo, los barceloneses consideraron las obras de Gaudí curiosidades de la historia de la arquitectura. No fue hasta que despertaron el interés sobre todo de los turistas japoneses que el maestro del modernismo catalán adquirió una nueva consideración entre los barceloneses.

Si La Rambla es la aorta de la ciudad y el Eixample la tarjeta de visita del modernismo, entonces el Barrio Gótico es el corazón de Barcelona. Es aquí donde los romanos fundaron su «colonia», su ciudad, desde entonces la administración municipal está ubicada aquí. Un gato dormita al sol, disfruta del calor de los ladrillos. Jaboneros, sombrereros, orfebres al lado de pequeñas tascas, panaderías y cafés (uno se puede perder por los estrechos callejones pero resulta agradable). Es agradable, pero no es museístico. Pese al Palacio Real donde Colón fue recibido en 1943 tras regresar de su viaje de descubrimiento del Nuevo Mundo. Y pese a la catedral gótica en cuya pila bautismal fueron bautizados seis indios que el descubridor trajo de su viaje.

Quien consiga ver la fachada de la catedral puede considerarse afortunado. Casi siempre está escondida detrás de andamios. Frente a su portada principal, sobre todo los domingos por la mañana, se bailan sardanas. Los amantes de este baile se cogen de las manos y sin apenas moverse del sitio dan pequeños pasos en círculo. Tienen cabida tanto para los turistas como para los barceloneses. En la época de Franco, el baile fue prohibido por ser la expresión del sentimiento de pertenencia catalán.

Aún así, se bailaba, y es que la anarquía es parte de la historia de la ciudad. De hecho, el 19 de julio de 1936 estaba previsto inaugurar los Juegos Olímpicos en Barcelona. La respuesta de la izquierda europea a la olimpiada celebrada en Berlín. Pero al amanecer, el pueblo se levantó contra las tropas del General Franco. Empieza la Guerra Civil. Tras dos días de lucha callejera sangrienta, los trabajadores, bajo la dirección del legendario Buenaventura Durruti, consiguen derrotar a los militares golpistas. El sindicato anarquista CNT, Confederación Nacional del Trabajo, entorno al que se habían organizado casi todos los trabajadores de la ciudad, domina todo el verano. Posteriormente son rigurosamente perseguidos por Franco, pero el recuerdo de la euforia y los ideales de aquellos días han pervivido hasta hoy.

Más antiguo, mucho más que el Eixample, es el barrio de la Barceloneta, situado en una lengua de la dársena. El barrio se construyó en 1719, cuando el Borbón Felipe V quería una ciudadela. Los habitantes fueron desplazados a la fuerza a la Barceloneta. Desde entonces, aquí viven mayoritariamente pescadores y trabajadores del puerto. La gente se conoce. O se conocía. Y es que cada vez son más los forasteros acomodados que descubren el atractivo de la Barceloneta y se establecen en esta lengua de tierra.

Cuando los Juegos Olímpicos, Barcelona se abrió al mar y la Barceloneta ganó una playa de un kilómetro de largo, poblada por las mañanas de jubilados curtidos por el sol que libran duelos de ajedrez en mesas de camping.

Por el paseo marítimo pasean jóvenes madres camino de la Vila Olímpica, con su símbolo, la escultura de una sardina gigante embarrancada, cuyas escamas de filamento de bronce brillan con el sol. Una obra del arquitecto Frank Gehry. Los dos edificios más altos de España dominan la Vila Olímpica: el de la aseguradora Mapfre y el del Hotel Arts. Pero hasta los años ochenta el litoral ofrecía otro aspecto, era una zona industrial. En aquella época los barceloneses sólo podían soñar con una casa de playa con palmeras, bares y cafés a la orilla del mar.

En el puerto también está la Torre de Sant Sebastià, el teleférico rojo que atraviesa el puerto hasta Montjuïc, la montaña local de Barcelona, y la zona verde más grande a la redonda. Al mismo tiempo, Montjuïc siempre fue la «matrona», en palabras del poeta catalán Jacint Verdaguer: de las distintas canteras de Montjuïc proviene el material de las murallas de Barcelona, casas e iglesias. Para la Exposición Universal de 1929 se construyeron parques y museos monumentales como el Palau Nacional, hoy, Museu Nacional d'Art de Catalunya; además de instalaciones deportivas, teatros y escenarios al aire libre. La colina se convirtió en área de reposo local, en pulmón verde. Sin embargo, la mejor vista de Barcelona no la ofrece Montjuïc, sino el fabuloso Parc Güell, tenía que ser una zona residencial ideada por Gaudí. Pero el dinero escaseó. Ha quedado un parque soñador con columnas y esculturas y un largo banco en forma de serpiente con trencadís (fragmentos cerámicos) de colores. A lo lejos se pueden ver las torres de la Sagrada Família, las calles ordenadas del Eixample, las hojas verdes de los plátanos de La Rambla. Mar, playa, árboles, casas, mosaicos: todo reluce. Barcelona brilla a la luz saturada de última hora de la tarde. Entre el mar y las montañas está la ciudad, incrustada como una joya. Historia esculpida a piedra y metrópolis moderna llena de vitalidad que jamás descansa.

Barcelona

Iris Lemanczyk

The sun rises up out of the sea, casting its shimmering blue light over La Rambla, the pulsating artery by day of this Catalan metropolis. A scene which caresses the spirit into wakefulness. The men of the cleaning gangs spray water from thick hoses. They clean up the leavings of the night from the corners of the main thoroughfares, making them clean and ready for the new day. The first trains begin to roll on the underground. The last night-revellers wend their way home.

If the day in Barcelona has any particular beginning, then it begins at half-past four in the morning in the Boqueria, the market hall in the inner city. Boqueria, an old Catalan word, is supposed to mean the "square where goat meat is sold". Today it is not only goat meat which is offered for sale. The iron roof also shelters one of the largest fish markets in Europe. From here, tonnes of seafood every day find their way into the cooking pots and pans of the pleasure-loving inhabitants of Barcelona. Thousands of smells, sometimes pleasant, although sometimes also enough to turn up one's nose, arouse the appetite, or at least curiosity, here in the stomach of Barcelona: Mussels, prawns and lobsters, pigs' trotters, black pudding, bacon and stewing fowl and truffles. Canarian bananas, olives, pistachios, fava beans and tomatoes, pigeons, rabbits, stockfish and silver giant eels. In the Boqueria, every customer - whether 17 or 70 years old – is a queen, a princess or a child. Men are addressed as "My heart's blood" or "My lovely". In the midst of the hustle and bustle, at the tapas stand "Pinocho", the chefs of the good restaurants hold an early morning meeting over a "café con leche" and discuss the offers of the day.

On the Rambla, the first street artists are putting on their make-up, turning themselves with outlandish costumes into silent, almost motionless angels, kings, Indians and even Batman. Fortune-tellers wait for business, while mime artists, fire-eaters, jugglers and musicians use the shady avenue of plane trees as a stage. A twelve hundred metre catwalk, crowds, the fear of pick-pockets, a multi-cultural happening, street-traders shouting the odds, undefinable noise, unique moments …

Rambla means a dried-up riverbed, which is used as a road. And this is exactly what La Rambla was. Following the demolition of the city wall, the first palaces of the nobility were constructed here, while the plane trees, which contribute so much to the pleasant atmosphere, were first planted in the 19th Century. The Rambla consists of several sections: the Rambla de Canaletes, the Rambla dels Estudis, the Rambla Sant Josep, the Rambla dels Caputxins and the Rambla Santa Mònica.

On weekdays from twelve to one, the pensioners gather around the iron fountain of the Font de Canaletes on the Rambla de Canaletes. Like the pigeons strutting around the waste-paper baskets, they pick up the latest results, rumours and newspaper reports about their football club, FC Barcelona. They discuss, speculate and share with each other a comforting feeling of satisfaction, when they have finally worked out their team's lead over Real Madrid. The joy of the fans is not only of a sporting nature, because every victory of "Barça" on the football field is simultaneously a triumph of the autonomous region of Catalonia over Madrid. This is a matter of honour and humiliation. More than anything else, the club is a symbol of the struggle of the Catalonians against the central government in Madrid. Not winning the league is bad, but finishing behind Real Madrid is a catastrophe. In the stadium therefore, "Barcelo-

nism" reaches its height, particularly in the match against their arch-rivals, a mixture of cosmopolitan striving for independence and chauvinistic arrogance, strangely mixed with "seny", healthy commonsense, and "rauxa", or creative chaos, but also hotheadedness and cheerfulness.
If "rauxa" is actually responsible for creativity, then Barcelona is richly blessed with this gift. Like a conjuror, the city tirelessly changes its appearance. At two world exhibitions and the 1992 Olympic Games, Barcelona every time made use of the opportunity to grow beyond its boundaries, to renovate ageing city districts and smarten itself up with new splendour. The concentration! The tempo! Anyone who saw the city before the games can only rub their eyes in disbelief. This most southern city of the north, or most northern city of the south, combining Mediterranean joy of life with big-city productivity. And nature also imposes strict limits on Barcelona. Hemmed in between the sea, the nearby mountain of Montjuïc and the foothills of the Serra de Collserola, room for further settlement is in short supply.
More than the usual "rauxa" can be found in the Eixample district and in the architectural works of Antoni Gaudí. During the course of the 19th Century, Barcelona threatened to burst at the seams. The city began to spread out until it covered almost the whole plain, which sloped gently from the mountains to the sea. "Eixample", city expansion, was the name given to the new quarter, a modest name for what was later to become the most characteristic part of Barcelona. The engineer Ildefons Cerdà designed a district with a chessboard pattern of broad streets crossing each other at right angles. The rich citizenry built here, in order to escape the confines of the old town.
Then something unexpected happened. A few years after the start of the construction work – in the late 19th Century – a new architectural style developed in the city, which began its triumphal march known in Barcelona as Modernism, and throughout the rest of Europe as Art nouveau, Jugendstil or Modern Style. Modernism is characterised particularly by the strict, rational layout of the Eixample. Imaginative, boisterous, organic, full of magical curves, flourishes, ornaments and dreamlike colours. A make-believe world of stone. Bright and cheerful.
In Eixample, where for reasons of prestige, residents are prohibited from hanging out their washing on the street side, stands perhaps most famous building in the Modernist style: the Sagrada Família, the Church of the Holy Family. The work was never finished. Financed entirely by private donations, building work on the church began in 1882 as a conventional neo-Gothic construction. One year later, the architectural direction was taken over by the 31-year old Antoni Gaudí, who changed the plans again and again. The church became his life's work, and was to become a "sermon in stone". From 1911, Gaudí declined all further commissions and concentrated exclusively on the Sagrada Família, living on the construction site, living for the construction site. 43 years long. After the crypt and apse, Gaudí could only complete the imposing East façade, with its many statues, and the four 360 ft. high spires. In 1926, Gaudí was run over by a streetcar, and died due to lack of first aid. In his worn clothing, nobody recognised the master builder until it was too late.
Interrupted by the Spanish Civil War, the construction work was resumed again in 1952. Gaudí is supposed to have reckoned on a construction time of 200 years. Optimists hope that the work will be completed by 2020, although it may not be finished until 2040. Gaudí's architectural works were long considered by the local population at least as curiosities of architectural history. Only through the active interest of tourists, and particularly the Japanese, did the master of Catalonian Modernism achieve new regard amongst the residents of Barcelona.
If the Rambla forms the main artery of the city, and Eixample the calling card of Modernism, the heart of Barcelona must be the Barri Gòtic. Here the Romans founded their "colònia", their town, which has since been home to the city administration. A cat dozes peacefully in the sun, enjoying the warmth of the bricks. Soap boilers, milliners, goldsmiths, cheek by jowl with small bars, bakeries and cafés – in the narrow alleyways, it is easy to lose oneself, although still very pleasant experience. Pleasant, but not museum-like. Despite the Royal Palace, where Columbus was received in 1493 after returning from his voyage of discovery to

the New World. And despite the Gothic cathedrals, in whose fonts six Indians, who the explorer brought back from his voyage, were baptised. Anyone who catches a glimpse of the façade of the cathedral is fortunate, since it is usually concealed behind scaffolding. On most Sunday mornings, the Sardana is performed in front of the main door of the cathedral. The dancers hold hands, and move in a circle in small steps, moving almost unnoticeably. There is room for tourists as well as the people of Barcelona. During the Franco era, the dance was prohibited, because it expresses the feeling of the shared Catalonian identity.

The dance continued to be performed however, since anarchy is part of the city's history. On 19th July 1936, the popular Olympic Games were due to be opened in Barcelona. The response of the European Left to the Olympics being held in Berlin. But in the dawn light, the people rose up against the troops of Generalísimo Franco – the spark that ignited the civil war. In two days of bloody street fighting, the workers under the leadership of the legendary Buenaventura Durruti succeeded in defeating the military putsch. One summer long the city was governed by the anarchistic trade union CNT, the Confederación Nacional del Trabajo, in which almost all the workers of the city were organised. They were later rigorously persecuted under Franco, but the memory of the euphoria and the ideals of this time remain alive to the present-day.

The city district of Barceloneta on a headland in the harbour is much, much older than the Eixample. The quarter grew up in 1719, when the Bourbon King Philipp V wanted to have a citadel. The residents were forcibly resettled to Barceloneta. Since then the district has been inhabited mainly by fishermen and port workers. People know each other, or at least they used to, because more and more wealthy strangers are now discovering the attraction of Barceloneta and moving onto the headland.

For the Olympic Games, Barcelona opened itself up to the sea, and Barceloneta was given a kilometre-long sandy beach, which is populated in the mornings by brown-tanned pensioners, sitting at camping tables playing chess.

On the beach promenade, young mothers stroll to the Olympic Village, with its trademark, a sculpture of a giant, stranded sardine, whose scales made of bronze wire glitter in the sun. A work by the architect Frank Gehry. The village is dominated by the two tallest buildings in Spain: the Mapfre Insurance Institute and the Hotel Arts. Even as late as the 1980's, the coast looked completely different, and was an industrial area. At that time, the people of Barcelona could only dream of their own beach, of palms, bars and cafés direct on the sea.

Also in the harbour stands the Torre de Sant Sebastià, the red cable car railway, which runs right across the harbour basin to the Montjuïc, Barcelona's "local hill" and the largest green space far and wide. The Montjuïc has also always been Barcelona's "proud mother", as the Catalan poet Jacint Verdaguer put it: from the innumerable quarries on the Montjuïc comes the material for Barcelona's city walls, houses and churches. For the 1929 World Exhibition, parks and monumental museums were constructed, such as the Palau Nacional, today's Museum of Catalan Art. Together with sports facilities, theatres and open-air stages. The hill became a local leisure area, the green lung of the city. But the most beautiful panorama over Barcelona is offered not from the Montjuïc, but from the fairytale Parc Güell, which was to become part of a residential complex designed by Gaudí. But funds ran short. There remains only a dream-like park with columns and sculptures, and a long curved bench covered in broken ceramics. From afar can be seen the spires of the Sagrada Família, the orderly streets of Eixample and the green leaves of the plane trees lining the Rambla. Sea, sand, trees, houses, mosaics – everything shines. Barcelona radiates in the rich light of the early evening. The city lies like a jewel set between the mountains and the sea. History hewn in stone and modern metropolis full of the lust for life. All round the clock.

Casa Milà

1

BE OPEN
EVERY SEASON

Santa Maria del Mar

Port del Fòrum

Edifici Fòrum

Museu d'Art Contemporani de Barcelona

Museu d'Art Contemporani de Barcelona

Torre de Telecomunicacions

Platja de la Barceloneta

Port Olímpic

Hotel Arts, La Barceloneta

Moll de les Balears i Torre de St. Sebastià

COMANAV

Monument a Cristòfol Colom

gasNatu

6 B 7
10 B 11
12 B 13
renfe

Estadi Camp Nou

MÉS QUE
UN CLUB

Cafe „Els Quatre Gats“

Per anar am bicicleta
no's pot du l'esquena dreta
R. Casas
4CATS

La Biblioteca de Catalunya

ad láter

Plaça del Rei

Carrer de l'Hospital

4
MORE
2
gravity

Hotel Comtes de Barcelona

Plaça d'Espanya i Palau Nacional

Nuclear Cardiology and Cardiac CT
10-13 May 2009
ServiFira
ENTRADA
90
ANYS
VIVINT
Acces Oficines
Acceso Oficinas
Office Entrance
RACC
90 saló del automòbil BARCELONA
1919/2009
ENTRADA
RACC
ENTRADA
ENTRADA
ENTRADA
ENTRADA

Hotel Hesperia Tower

Barri Gòtic

Banc de Trencadís, Parc Güell

BAR
RESTAURANT

Parc Güell

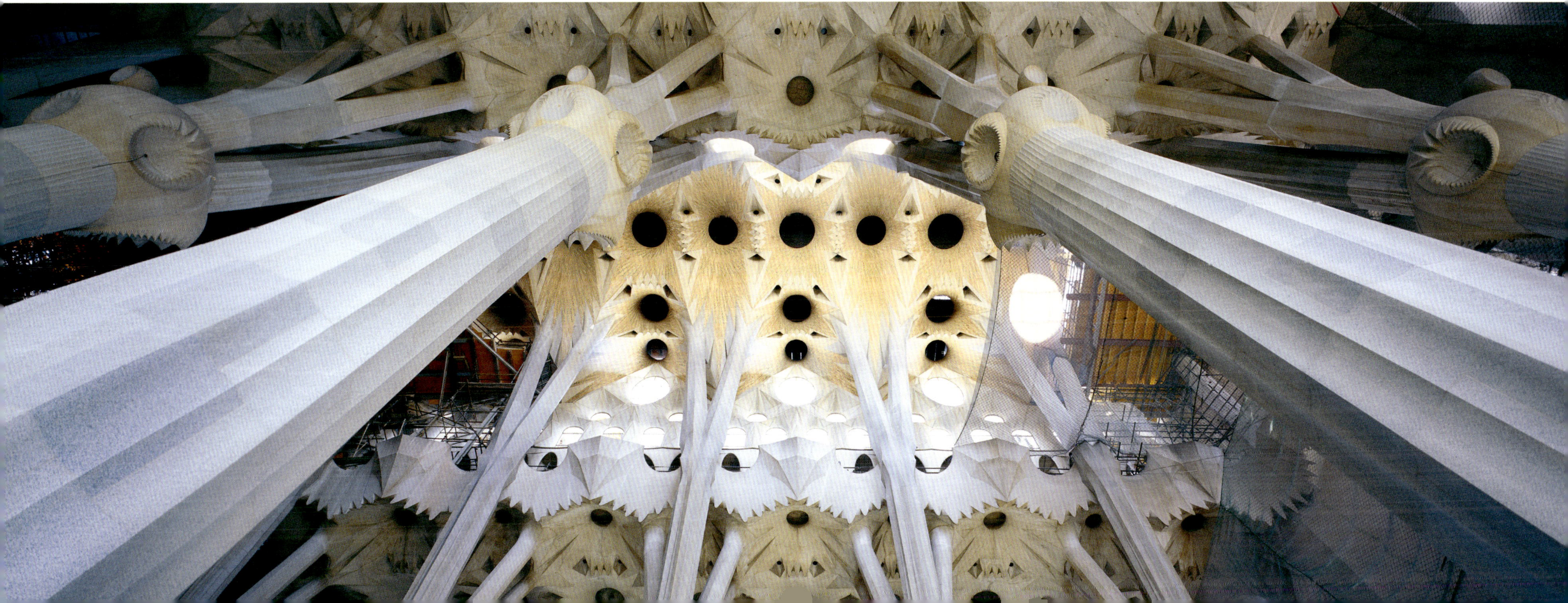

COMANAV

Carrer del Bisbe Irurita

vodafone

Barcelona

www.micha-pawlitzki.com

MICHA PAWLITZKI, Jahrgang 1972, machte sich während seines Studiums der Betriebswirtschaft als Photograph selbständig. Bis zum Abschluss seiner Promotion war er als wissenschaftlicher Mitarbeiter am Lehrstuhl für Personalmanagement der Universität Augsburg tätig. Seit 2005 arbeitet Micha Pawlitzki ausschließlich als Photograph und hat bereits über 80 Bücher und Kalender veröffentlicht. Er ist bei den beiden größten Bildagenturen der Welt unter Vertrag. Micha Pawlitzki reist vier bis fünf Monate im Jahr um die Welt, immer auf der Suche nach neuen Motiven, unentdeckten Orten, dem besten Licht und einzigartigen Perspektiven. Er lebt mit seiner Frau Melanie in Augsburg.

IRIS LEMANCZYK wurde 1964 in Kirchheim/Teck bei Stuttgart geboren. Nach dem Studium der Germanistik und Geographie lockte immer wieder die Ferne. Sie reiste um die Welt, schnupperte eine Zeit lang Zirkusluft, lebte in Namibia und besuchte für ein paar Monate Australien und Neuseeland. Dazwischen arbeitete sie als Zeitungs-Redakteurin bei der „Südwest Presse" in Ulm. Seit 1997 ist sie freiberuflich tätig, schreibt Kinder- und Jugendbücher sowie Sachbücher, verfasst Reiseberichte und ist als Dozentin für Kreatives Schreiben tätig.

MICHA PAWLITZKI va començar a treballar com a fotògraf free-lance mentre estudiava Ciències Empresarials i de seguida va publicar els primers llibres de fotografies i calendaris. En acabar els estudis, va treballar de professor i va fer el doctorat en Psicologia de la Publicitat; des del 2005 es dedica exclusivament a la fotografia. A llarg d'aquest temps ha publicat més de 70 llibres i calendaris amb les seves imatges. Micha Pawlitzki treballa per a totes les agències de fotografia de renom i cada any passa entre quatre i cinc mesos viatjant. Viu amb la seva dona Melanie a Augsburg.

IRIS LEMANCZYK va néixer a Kirchheim/Teck, prop de Stuttgart, el 1964. La llunyania l'atreia cada cop més, i en acabar els seus estudis en Filologia Germànica i Geografia va emprendre un viatge per tot el món, va tastar un temps la vida del circ, va viure a Namíbia i va passar uns mesos a Austràlia i Nova Zelanda. Entre un viatge i un altre, va treballar com a redactora de diari per a la publicació Südwest Presse d'Ulm. Des del 1997 es dedica a escriure llibres infantils i juvenils així com llibres especialitzats, redacta reportatges de viatge i ensenya escriptura creativa.

MICHA PAWLITZKI empezó a trabajar como fotógrafo independiente en 1995, mientras todavía estaba estudiando Ciencias Empresariales. Poco después publicó sus primeros calendarios y volúmenes ilustrados, que fueron seguidos por exposiciones de sus instantáneas. Tras terminar su carrera trabajó entre 1999 y 2004 –hasta finalizar los estudios de doctorado– de asistente de investigación en la Cátedra de Gerencia de Personal de la Universidad de Augsburgo. Micha Pawlitzki trabaja desde 2005 exclusivamente de fotógrafo. Hasta ahora ya han salido a la luz más de 70 libros y calendarios con sus fotografías. Cuando no se encuentra realizando algunas de sus giras fotográficas por el extranjero, Micha Pawlitzki reside y trabaja con su esposa Melanie en Augsburgo.

IRIS LEMANCZYK nació en 1964 en el pueblo de Kirchheim/Teck junto a Stuttgart (Alemania). Tras terminar su carrera de Filología Germánica y Geografía se dejó atraer cada vez más por el encanto de los destinos exóticos: viajó por el mundo, experimentó durante algún tiempo la vida en un circo, residió en Namibia y pasó algunos meses en Australia y Nueva Zelanda. Y entre todas esas ocupaciones todavía encontró tiempo para aprender un oficio serio: redactora de periódicos en la editorial alemana "Südwest Presse" de Ulm. Desde 1997 trabaja como redactora libre y escribe diversos libros: desde literatura infantil y juvenil a libros de texto. Además confecciona relatos de viaje e imparte seminarios de creación literaria.

MICHA PAWLITZKI, while completing his degree in business administration, started working professionally as a photographer in 1995. Soon he published his first coffee table books and calendars. After finishing his PhD and working as assistant professor he has been working fulltime as a photographer since 2005. He has published more than 70 books and calendars. Micha Pawlitzki works for all renowned stock photo agencies and travels abroad four to five months every year working on his photographic projects. He lives in Augsburg with his wife Melanie.

IRIS LEMANCZYK was born in 1964 in Kirchheim/Teck near Stuttgart. After studying German and geography, she gave way to the call of far-distant places. She travelled around the world, experienced the circus life for a time, lived in Namibia and spent several months in Australia and New Zealand. In between, she also learnt something more conventional: newspaper editing with the "Südwest Presse" in Ulm. Since 1997 she has worked as a freelancer, writing children's books and non-fiction and compiling travel reports, and also works as a lecturer on creative writing.

In der EDITION PANORAMA BIBLIOTHEK erhältlich | Disponible a la col·lecció EDITION PANORAMA BIBLIOTHEK | Tambien disponible en la EDITION PANORAMA BIBLIOTHEK | Available in the EDITION PANORAMA BIBLIOTHEK

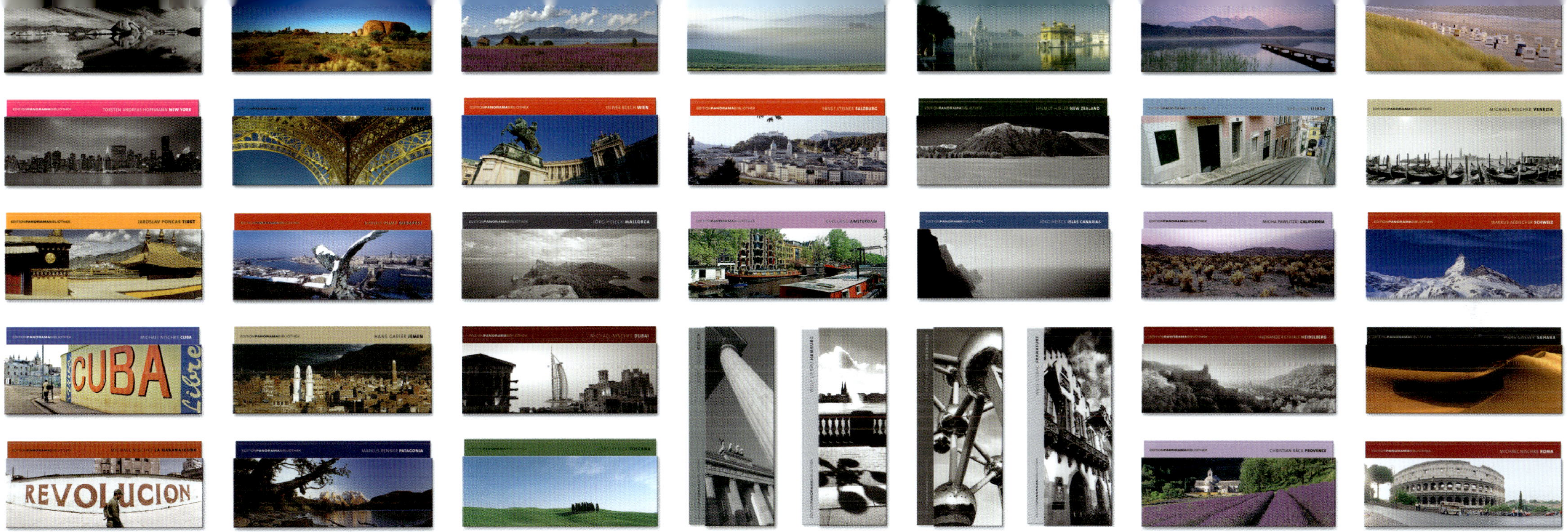

Iceland	978-3-89823-189-5
New York	978-3-89823-392-7
Tibet	978-3-89823-197-8
Cuba	978-3-89823-355-2
La Habana, Cuba	978-3-89823-179-4
Australia	978-3-89823-284-5
Paris	978-3-89823-239-5
Budapest	978-3-89823-280-7
Jemen	978-3-89823-278-4
Patagonia	978-3-89823-360-6
Norway	978-3-89823-393-4
Wien	978-3-89823-380-4
Mallorca	978-3-89823-290-6
Dubai	978-3-89823-279-1
Toscana	978-3-89823-198-5
Schwarzwald	978-3-89823-395-8
Salzburg	978-3-89823-394-1
Amsterdam	978-3-89823-353-8
Berlin	978-3-89823-168-8
Hamburg	978-3-89823-283-8
India	978-3-89823-237-1
New Zealand	978-3-89823-359-0
Islas Canarias	978-3-89823-357-6
Bruxelles	978-3-89823-354-5
Frankfurt	978-3-89823-390-3
Österreich	978-3-89823-381-1
Lisboa	978-3-89823-358-3
California	978-3-89823-389-7
Heidelberg	978-3-89823-356-9
Provence	978-3-89823-409-2
Sylt	978-3-89823-363-7
Venezia	978-3-89823-238-8
Schweiz	978-3-89823-362-0
Sahara	978-3-89823-183-1
Roma	978-3-89823-361-3

A production by EDITION PANORAMA, Germany

Printed in Germany

EDITION PANORAMA GmbH
G7, 14
D-68159 Mannheim
Telefon +49 (0)621 / 32 88 69 - 0
Fax +49 (0)621 / 32 88 69 - 20
info@editionpanorama.com
www.editionpanorama.com

ISBN: 978-3-89823-410-8

Concept: Bernhard & Sebastian Wipfler
Design: EDITION PANORAMA | Diana May
Designgruppe Fanz & Neumayer | Marcus Bela Schmitt
Editorial department: Dr. Christophe Klimmer, Wolfgang Roth
Translations: Global-Text, Heidelberg | Mercè Amat Riera, Mark Woolfe
Separations: EPS GmbH, Speyer
Printing: abcdruck GmbH, Heidelberg
Printed on Profimatt, produced by Sappi – exclusive by Igepagroup
Bookbinding: Josef Spinner Großbuchbinderei GmbH, Ottersweier
Covermaterial: "Imperial" Book Cloth, BN International
Endpapers: "Freelife Merida Graphite" 140 g/m², Fedrigoni Group
Slipcase: Neudel Verpackungen GmbH, Neckarbischofsheim